MARINE LIFE
OF THE
CARIBBEAN

MARINE LIFE OF THE CARIBBEAN

Photography by
James Cribb

Text by
Jacques-Yves Cousteau
and
Thomas H. Suchanek

SKYLINE PRESS

To Andrea, Jessica and Michaela

Produced by Roger Boulton Publishing Services, Toronto
Designed by Fortunato Aglialoro

ISBN 0-19-540616-8
1 2 3 4 – 7 6 5 4

Printed in Hong Kong by Scanner Art Services, Inc., Toronto

Preface

Here I am three hundred miles off the coast of Ecuador steaming towards the Galapagos archipelago, and sitting on deck to write this note for a book on the marine life of the Caribbean. It seems odd somehow—the other sea so far away. Yet I sit here, on a still ocean in the equatorial sun, the occasional flying fish off to starboard, and the Caribbean memories are vivid still. We anchored over a reef, my wife Andrea and I, dropped down into the silence, through water so clear—it was our first sight of the Caribbean below the waves. Something of that time and many like it since is in these pages. They will suggest, perhaps, the sense of wonder, even of awe, and the serenity that comes upon me whenever I enter those depths. We needs must see this fragile undersea life as infinitely precious to us and future generations; I recall some words of Bahá'u'lláh, 'O wayfarer in the path of God! Take thou thy portion of the ocean of His grace and deprive not thyself of the things that lie hidden in its depths.' The most eloquent words would fall short in describing the wonder that greeted us on our first descent into those waters and again for many months to follow. Here instead is a sampling of what we saw.

I am especially proud that M. Jacques-Yves Cousteau consented to write a foreword to this book, not only because his eminent name is synonymous around the world with oceanic conservation but because of his invaluable efforts in gaining protected status for Ile de Pigeon in the Caribbean. While we were working on the photography for this book Andrea and I lived in a small fishing hamlet close to Ile de Pigeon on the island of Guadeloupe and the abundant marine life there was a most wonderful experience for us. The association of M. Cousteau with this book recalls a place and time of great delight.

The captions to the photographs are the result of long and dedicated labour by Dr Thomas H. Suchanek, Research Associate at the University of California. With the photographs as his only reference Tom undertook the formidable task of identifying the creatures depicted, out of the infinite variety of underwater species. The frequent use of such words as 'unidentifiable,' 'probably,' and 'most likely' indicates that exact identification may not always be possible on visual information alone. Precise identification may demand that a creature be touched or even chemically analysed, or that its life-stage be first determined. Nonetheless, information such as is contained in these captions brings an essential and fascinating element to the worth of any book of this kind.

In addition to M. Cousteau and Dr Suchanek I must thank my wife Andrea for her support both in and out of the water; my parents, Jean and Jack Cribb, and Betty and Des Clements, for sending on the necessary packages of film and equipment; Peter Dickinson, for the many dives we logged together; Paul Coulon, for his advice and diving gear; the Baha'i pioneers of Guadeloupe; Roger Boulton, for producing this book; and the people of Deshaies, Guadeloupe, for the affection and hospitality they showed to Andrea and myself throughout our lengthy stay.

JAMES CRIBB

Introduction

The Caribbean Sea is encircled by two continents and by the arc of islands comprising the Greater and Lesser Antilles. It is thus a semi-enclosed basin and has often been compared to the Mediterranean, but the likeness is only superficial. To understand fully the nature of this extraordinary sea one must become familiar with the people who live around her shores, with the gentle tradewinds and the devastating hurricanes that move across her waters, with the currents that bring nutrients from other liquid realms, and with the magnificent creatures that enliven her depths.

On board our research ship *Calypso* I have often sailed the Caribbean. My colleagues and I have made hundreds of memorable dives with aqualungs and exploration submarines. We have lowered instruments to measure the physical factors that would encourage or inhibit life. We have involved fishermen, farmers, businessmen and political leaders in our researches. By way of exhaustive studies we came to the sad conclusion that the natural resources and treasures of beauty so artistically portrayed in this book by James Cribb were threatened by the rapidly growing population of the surrounding countries and by careless exploitation of the Caribbean Sea.

The waters of the Caribbean have three origins—the clean, pure waters from the tropical Atlantic, pushed through the eastern string of islands by the western oceanic currents and the trade winds; the turbid but rich waters from the mighty Amazon and Orinoco rivers, driven into the straits between Trinidad and Grenada by a powerful ocean current; and the clean, rich waters that have travelled all the way from the Antarctic along the bottom of the Atlantic, and that *Calypso* clearly identified when we were making a survey along the coasts of Venezuela. This exceptional cocktail of waters enters the Caribbean Sea and feeds the main Caribbean currents that turn clockwise, bathing successively the coasts of Venezuela, Colombia, Central America, the Yucatán Peninsula of Mexico, Cuba, Jamaica, Haiti and the Dominican Republic. The nutrients carried by this current are progressively depleted as they are fed upon by the local marine creatures. The underwater splendors that have been laboriously created through millions of years of evolution and struggle for survival are in fact highly vulnerable.

One of the most spectacular features of the Caribbean is the coral structure extending along the coast of Belize. This is the second largest barrier reef of the planet, second in size only to the world-renowned barrier reef of Australia. In several places the coral wall is indented by steep valleys where fish congregate to spawn. We have witnessed the mating frenzy of groupers, coming there by the tens of thousands—nobody knows from where—for ceremonies that reminded me of the nuptial dances of birds such as cranes. Groupers are able to change sex, becoming alternately males or females. In the crevices of the Belize reefs clouds of these fairly large fish separate into pairs, each couple spinning close to another in frantic rhythm, changing color from the usual brown to silvery white and purplish red, and totally unaware of the predatory crowd of local fishermen.

While the acts of procreation were performed in a hundred feet of depth, while fertilized eggs were released in the current to be disseminated afar, dozens of small boats, attracted by the seasonal bonanza, were lowering hooks and lines and taking tons of groupers on board. Still alive, the fish were stored in pens built of reeds in shallow waters and were kept ready to be sent to market on demand. The *Calypso* divers remained on the spot for several weeks, shooting film and admiring the beauty of the natural show as long as the mating went on. Then the couples became fewer, the animation faded out, until the last grouper left and the reef seemed like a desert to us, though it was still alive with the usual motley population of butterfly fish and other reef creatures.

The shallow part of the Belize reef is connected in several places to freshwater streams and to marshes from which manatees sometimes venture in search of seaweeds and probably seeking warmer waters in which to give birth to their cubs. On the windward side of the great barrier the coral cliff drops rather abruptly and down in the twilight zone tall, brown, branching trees called 'black coral' grow here and there. In fact the trunk and the branches are not made of limestone, like coral heads, but of a horny material like sea fans or gorgonians. Black coral trees, usually surrounded by clouds of damselfish, are a breathtaking sight. Unfortunately black coral is a precious material. When stripped of its natural brown fleshy coating it can be carved and polished into shining, handsome objects or sculptures. It is in great demand in Muslim countries for making costly prayer beads. As a result of its value, black coral is sought after by adventurous divers; because of the depths at which it grows and because it is extremely hard to saw or uproot, divers stay down too long at these dangerous depths and often suffer severe decompression accidents. At the same time the black coral itself has really become an endangered species.

Another exciting area lies along the northern coast of Jamaica. Near Montego Bay there are superb coral reefs, of the fringed reef type, that are split by deep but narrow corridors meandering far into the majestic structure, built over millions of years by the tiny Pharaos of the sea. For weeks I have enjoyed diving slowly along the exiguous fractures, deep into walls one hundred feet high, carved by caves, winding abruptly in hairpin curves. The fantasy of shapes was blending perfectly with an explosion of colors as soon as I aimed my lamps onto Nature's most artistic display; but the exuberance of the show was hiding perpetual tragedies. It was there in Jamaica that, with the help of local scientists, we could observe, photograph and film the endless struggle of some species of coral for vital space. The beautiful polyps were cannibals, slowly devouring their neighbours in order to expand their own colony. Everywhere the splendor of the sight was covering up the ugliness of an increasing war for survival.

Nature's harsh rules applied also to humans. While diving in Jamaica's coral paradise I had wondered at the virtual absence of fish. The natural tenants of the colorful gardens, butterfly fish, liar fish, doctorfish, angelfish and others such had disappeared. Hardly could we spot a few damselfish or a couple of clownfish sheltered in their stinging anemonae. I found out the explanation by talking to old fishermen while they were hoisting their fish-traps of wirenetting. The mesh were smaller than one half of an inch. Inside the traps the harvest was meagre; a few, very small, reef fish. The men told me that over the years they had been obliged to use smaller and smaller mesh in order to catch anything at all. They knew they were jeopardising the future but, they told me sadly, they had no choice, they were poor, and they had to eat.

With exploding populations all around the Caribbean the same imperative, survival, was slowly but surely exhausting the very resource that humans depended upon. If the sea was to be restored to its natural wealth the current game of 'catch as catch can' would have to be abandoned and drastic, unconventional solutions would have to be found and implemented.

We came across another man-made problem in Venezuela. In a vast expanse, between Trinidad, the Lesser Antilles, and the coast of the mainland, there thrives a resident pack of whales, together with manta rays, dolphins and sharks. Fast hydrofoil boats have been imported from Italy to carry passengers to the island of Margarita. Several times these boats, speeding at 35 knots on their sharp underwater wings, have collided with whales and suffered serious damage. The reaction of the shipowners was to suggest the destruction of the whales. Fortunately the authorities have not complied. . .yet.

Another interesting spot in the Caribbean is the Alacran Reef, an isolated coral structure where many ships ran ashore and litter the treacherous shallows. Several shipwrecks still raise their steel skeletons above the raging surf. Diving among mazes of jagged rusty plates is a dangerous but exciting sport. Schools of jacks play with the alternating currents created by the pounding waves. Spiny lobsters hide in metal recesses. Broken plates and decaying artefacts litter the ships' remains.

Off the Yucatán Peninsula, at the island of Contoy, we witnessed the mysterious migration of the spiny lobsters. In December they gather by the thousands, concealed in little groups under every stone. They seem to be waiting for a signal, and this long-awaited signal is the first northern gale after Christmas. Then they all come out, line up in long processions, and walk ceremoniously towards the southeast until they disappear. The destination of this huge migration is still unknown, despite considerable research by scientists. Of course fishermen take advantage of this phenomenon and in two days tons of lobsters are captured, deep-frozen, and sent to marketplaces in America and Europe. The mass slaughter is a bonanza for fishermen but it is believed to endanger the future of the spiny lobster.

A very unusual adventure awaits divers in the Caribbean off St Pierre, on the west coast of Martinique. On 8 May 1902 the volcano towering over the city, 'La Montagne Pelée', exploded, completely destroying St Pierre, killing all 30,000 inhabitants save one (a prisoner protected by the thick stone walls of his tiny cell), and sinking seventeen ships offshore. Today St Pierre is alive again but not all the scars have healed, and the population is five times smaller than it was before the explosion. The sunken ships lie strewn about the bottom of the bay, at depths ranging from ten to ninety metres, covered with coral, sea fans and algae, and occupied by resident and visiting fish.

The most beautiful of those wrecks, the *Roraima*, lies 165 feet down. She remains an impressive ship even after more than 80 years, with her tall, proud bow, her gangways, her engine, her steering system. She was set ablaze by the incandescent cloud of gases from the exploding volcano, and I found on board a bottle that had melted in the heat of that inferno. Today it is covered with colorful growth and with the long pale virgularians that account for the nickname given to the *Roraima* by divers—'the white-hair wreck'.

On the other side of the island at Le Robert a successful fish farm makes a 'contract of hope' with the ships' cemetery of St Pierre. Thanks to the collaboration of enlightened citizens, of scientists and of the local fishermen, an experimental enterprise of aquaculture is demonstrating that it is technically and economically feasible to raise tons of commercial fish, such as bass, in an impoverished marine environment. If such endeavours are soon more widespread the output of fish farms will not only contribute to the sustenance of hungry people but will also reduce the excessive pressure recently applied to the natural richness and diversity of Caribbean marine life.

JACQUES-YVES COUSTEAU

1 A diver hovers over a dead Star coral *(Montastrea)* head, overgrown by assorted tubular sponges like the brown one shown, of the genus *Verongia*.

2 *(left)* Chromis (the identifiable fish here are the Brown chromis, *Chromis multilineatus*), which are planktivores (i.e.—they eat plankton), hanging over a reef with smooth brain coral, *Diploria strigosa* and a bushy gorgonian, *Plexaura flexuosa*; also a reddish colored Blackbar soldierfish, *Myripristis jacobus*, at lower left and the Yellowhead wrasse, *Halichoeres garnoti*, just to the right of the gorgonian.

3 A barrel sponge, *Xestospongia muta*, one of the largest of the Caribbean sponges. This sponge is hard and 'glassy' to the touch, crumbling under pressure; may reach 1.5 m high and wide and typically 'buttressed' as shown in photo. Normally occurs from about 10–120m depth.

4 One of the most common Caribbean
anemones, *Condylactis gigantea*. Tentacles may reach over 10 cm and their
tips may be pink as shown here, all
green like the rest of the tentacles, or
yellowish in color; usually found in
crevices and/or attached to pieces of
rubble.

5 A juvenile Queen angelfish, *Holocanthus ciliaris*. When mature they
lose the vertical blue bars and keep the blue margin.

6 *(left)* School comprised mostly of the conspicuous Yellowtail snapper, *Ocyurus chrysurus*, a plankton feeder. Often 'hangs' or cruises over reefs, feeding. A very common reef fish of the Caribbean. Highly regarded as a good eating fish. Reef comprised of the common finger coral, *Porites,* and sponges of the genus *Callyspongia* (foreground) and *Ircinia stobilina* (far left).

7 Two closely related Hydrozoan corals (in a totally different class—Hydrozoa—from most other reef corals, Anthozoa), the pink hydrocoral, *Stylaster roseus,* which usually inhabits cryptic (i.e.—cave-like) habitats, and the firecoral, *Millepora* (of the *M. alcicornis/complanata* complex—it is argued that all the growth forms may be the same species). In both corals, defensive polyps are sticking out (the thin thread-like hairs). Brushing against the firecorals will give a nasty sting and some people are allergic to them. The fish seen here are the Bluehead wrasse, *Thalassoma bifasciatum.* These particular individuals may be either male or female.

8 The sponge is most probably a *Verongia* sp., recognized by the typical tubular growth form for this genus. Fish are most probably more Chromis.

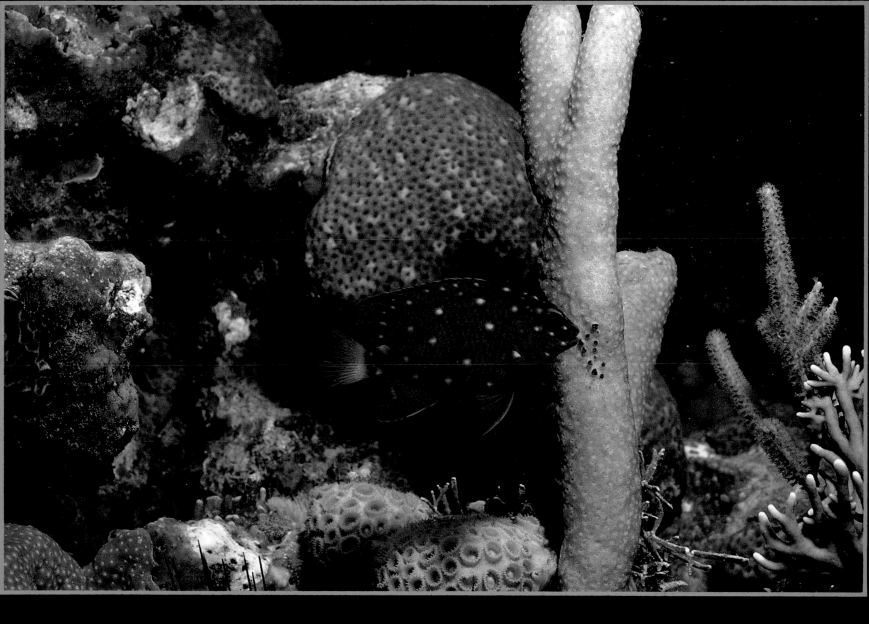

9 Juvenile of a Yellowtail damselfish, *Microspathodon chrysurus*. The adult body will be dark brown or black, but still with a yellow tail. Other name, 'jewelfish', comes from the jewel-like nature of the color patterns of the juvenile. Often hides among branches of firecoral, but here is shown in front of the Starlet coral, *Siderastrea* sp. and the retracted gorgonian, *Plexaurella* sp., with another gorgonian, *Eunicea* (maybe *laxispica*) to the far right with its feeding polyps extended.

0 Probably the most common coral in the Caribbean, the Elkhorn coral, *Acropora palmata*. Its polyps are usually out feeding at night—on plank-on, as it utilizes photosynthetic biproducts from its symbiotic algae zooxanthellae) during the day, as most reef corals do. This is one of the most important *framework* builders for all Caribbean reefs (along with *Montastrea annularis* see #1). This species, *A. palmata*, grows rapidly (sometimes reaching 10 cm/yr—which is a lot for a coral) but its branches are broken off during hurricanes and other bad storms that bring heavy wave action. The fish, again, are the common yellow form of the Bluehead wrasse (see #7)

1 Dominant adult male Bluehead wrasse *Thalassoma bifasciatum*.
Dominant, sexually mature males, often called *supermales*, are large and
have a brilliant blue head and green trunk. Supermales can be the result of
sex reversal in this species (i.e.—a female turns into a male) usually when
the existing dominant male is killed or dies—this process is called protandric hermaphroditism.

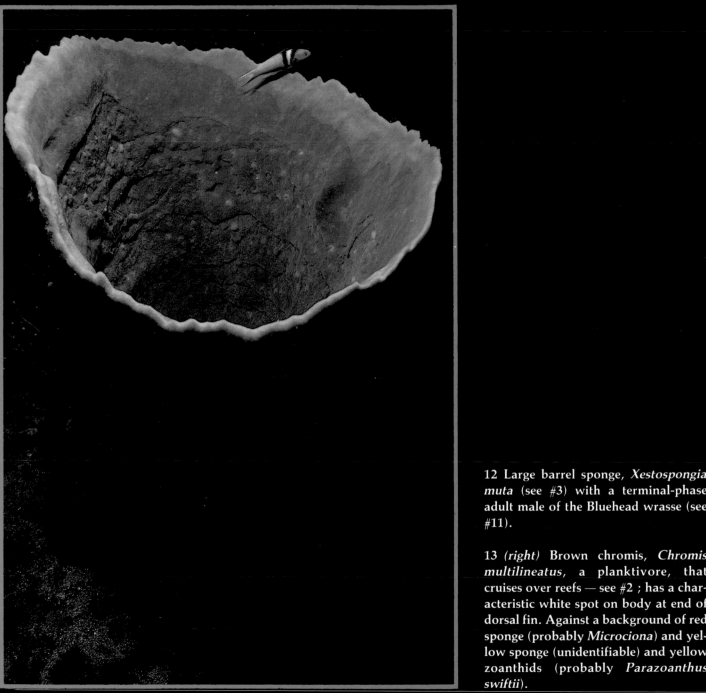

12 Large barrel sponge, *Xestospongia muta* (see #3) with a terminal-phase adult male of the Bluehead wrasse (see #11).

13 *(right)* Brown chromis, *Chromis multilineatus*, a planktivore, that cruises over reefs — see #2 ; has a characteristic white spot on body at end of dorsal fin. Against a background of red sponge (probably *Microciona*) and yellow sponge (unidentifiable) and yellow zoanthids (probably *Parazoanthus swiftii*).

14 *(left)* A Goldentail moray, *Muraena miliaris*; typically hides in a reef crevice, as most morays do; grows to about 50 cm in length. In general, nocturnal and mostly feeds on fishes. Large morays may be poisonous to eat.

15 The Sand diver (Lizardfish), *Synodus intermedius* grows to c. 45 cm,— swims in short spurts and then rests on bottom—a predator on other smaller fishes. Here seen resting against an unidentifiable sponge.

16 The plume-like gorgonian of the genus *Pseudopterogorgia* (possibly *P. americana*); colonies can reach over 1.5 m–1.8 m high. Branches are usually 'slimy' to the touch. Some yellow-phase Bluehead wrasses are hiding in amongst the branches (see #7).

17 The Graysby, *Petrometopon cruentatum* grows to about 30 cm, and is characterized by the row of spots (they can be black or white—here white) on back. Otherwise similar to a fish called a coney *(Cephalopholis fulva)* which always has 2 black spots on lower lip. Some fire coral at lower left.

18 The mustard-colored growth is fire-coral, *Millepora* (see #7). Red branched sponge is *Haliclona rubens*, a common reef inhabitant; branches may reach 40 cm in length. Color can vary from a dark brown to red to grey-brown to black. Anemone on the left is *Stoichactis helianthus*, with short, rounded and *very* sticky tentacles. Some people are sensitive to its stinging cells. A brittle-star (an ophiuroid) is wrapping its arms around the sponge and the firecoral in the background. Brittlestars often sit atop sponges and benefit from the sponges pumping water for them as they extract food particles from the water stream.

19 *(right)* Terminal-phase male Blue-head wrasse (see #7 & 11), over a red sponge (probably *Microciona*).

20 Gorgonian (*Pseudoplexaura* sp.) with the convoluted leaf coral, *Agaricia agaricites* in the foreground.

21 *(right)* Mixed school of planktivores comprised of 2 terminal-phase males of the Bluehead wrasse (see #7 & 11) and the Brown chromis (see #1 & 13). Upright gorgonian is possibly a *Pseudoplexaura*. Most of the yellow-colored coral seen here is the Yellow pencil coral, *Madracis mirabilis*. The black spines of the sea urchin, *Diadema antillarum* can be seen sticking out of the reef in the lower-center.

22 *(left)* The fish is the Trumpetfish, *Aulostomus maculatus*, which can grow to 90 cm and is a voracious sit-and-wait predator on smaller fish; hangs motionless in the water, sometimes upside-down, waiting for prey. It can change ▮or and camouflage itself by mimicking its background. Here the background is red and orange and pur-pl▮ ponges, the hydrocoral *Stylaster roseus* (see #7), the leaf coral, *Agaricia*, som▮ recoral and what look like some bus▮ hydroids.

23 Secretive by day, crinoids (closely related to sea urchins and starfish) are nocturnal plankton feeders that crawl out on a reef promontory (or extend arms through a crevice) by night to capture the abundant plankton that emerge from the reef. This species is called *Nemaster rubiginosa* and is rela-tively abundant and usually lives at depths of ▮0–30 m. Arms can be a variety of colors—sometimes orange with yellow tips or white with black tips. Here a crinoid sits at the base of the barrel sponge, *Xestospongia muta* (see ▮3 & 12). Another *Xestospongia* can be seen in the background.

24 *Polychaetes*, segmented marine worms in the group generally called serpulid worms, build calcareous (i.e.—limestone) tubes that descend down into the coral 'rock'. These worms have fantastically quick reactions and can retract into their tubes in a fraction of a second should they sense a pressure wave from an approaching object like a predator or a camera lens. Against red (again probably *Microciona*) and unidentifiable orange sponge.

25 In the foreground a mixture of various unidentifiable sponges, firecoral (lower left) and dead coral. The sea fan (gorgonian) is called *Gorgonia* (there are several species that all look very similar). These sea fans usually orient their growth at right angles to the current so as to intercept the maximum flow in order to extract plankton. The fish is the adult form of the Yellowtail damselfish, *Microspathodon chrysurus* (see #9).

26 Another plume-like gorgonian, *Pseudopterogorgia* sp. (see #16) hiding behind a couple of heads of the common Mountainous star coral, *Montastrea annularis*. At lower depth this coral is known to change its colony shape, becoming flattened and plate-like instead of mound-like in order to gather more sunlight for the symbiotic algae that are in its tissues). Orange sponge is unidentifiable. Faint traces of an urchin hiding in the center crevice and another crinoid *(Nemaster)* (see #23) sticking out from behind the star coral colony.

27 *(right)* Juvenile of the sea urchin, *Diadema antillarum* resting on a colony of the Mountainous star coral, *Montastrea annularis*. Young urchins of this particular species have white or black and white striped spines, which turn all black as adults. They scrape algae from coral-rock surfaces or eat seagrasses with a sophisticated series of 5 opposing teeth in a jaw apparatus called an Aristotle's Lantern. They are mostly nocturnal, hiding from predatory fishes by day.

28 *(left)* Trumpetfish, *Aulostomus maculatus* (see #22) against a red sponge (probably *Microciona*) and some yellow anemone-like animals called zoanthids *(Parazoanthus swiftii)* interspersed throughout the sponges and some *Agaricia* coral.

29 Juvenile of the common Threespot damselfish (also called Yellow damselfish). *Eupomacentrus planifrons* (note: the adults are dark overall with a yellowish tinge) against a backdrop of fire coral, *Millepora alcicornis* and what looks like a retracted gorgonian. Lower left coral is the Mustard coral, *Porites astreoides*.

30 Adult of the common French grunt, *Haemulon flavolineatum*. These grow to about 30 cm and gather in large schools by day. They eat small invertebrates, but here one has fallen prey to a parasite, the isopod *Anilocra* that has latched onto its left cheek. This large ectoparasite is a female, having been transformed from a much smaller male in the sex-reversal process called protandric hermaphroditism. Upper right is a sponge; behind center, a *Diadema* urchin; directly below are the extended polyps of an encrusting gorgonian, probably *Erythropodium caribaeorum*.

31 *(right)* A tiny blenny (probably a Saddled blenny, *Malacoctenus triangulatus*) in a hole in a 'brain' coral that is probably *Diploria strigosa*.

32 The Sharptail eel, *Myrichthys acuminatus* grows to 90 cm; usually found in seagrass beds, but obviously frequents reef areas too. Here seen next to the red sponge, *Haliclona rubens* on the left and the Cavernous star coral, *Montastrea cavernosa* on the right.

33 *(right)* A sea cucumber, possibly *Holothuria floridana or mexicana* below the Cavernous star coral, *Montastrea cavernosa*.

34 The Feather-duster worm, *Sabellas-tarte magnifica*, lives in a parchment-like, flexible tube and extends these tentacles to filter particles from the water column for food. Also has *very* quick retraction reactions like the ser-pulid worms in #24. Blue sponge below worm is unidentifiable.

35 *(right)* An adult of the Threespot (or Yellow) Damselfish, *Eupomacentrus planifrons* (see #29), hanging over what looks like the barrel sponge, *Xestos-pongia muta* (see #3 & 12).

36 The Porcupinefish, *Diodon hystrix*, can grow to 90 cm in length and is the largest of the porcupine group in the Caribbean. It can balloon-up with water to 2–3 times original size if frightened. This is an effective intimidation and anti-predation mechanism. Powerful beak-like teeth and crushing palates prey on sea urchins, molluscs (especially snails), and crabs. May reach as far north as Massachussetts.

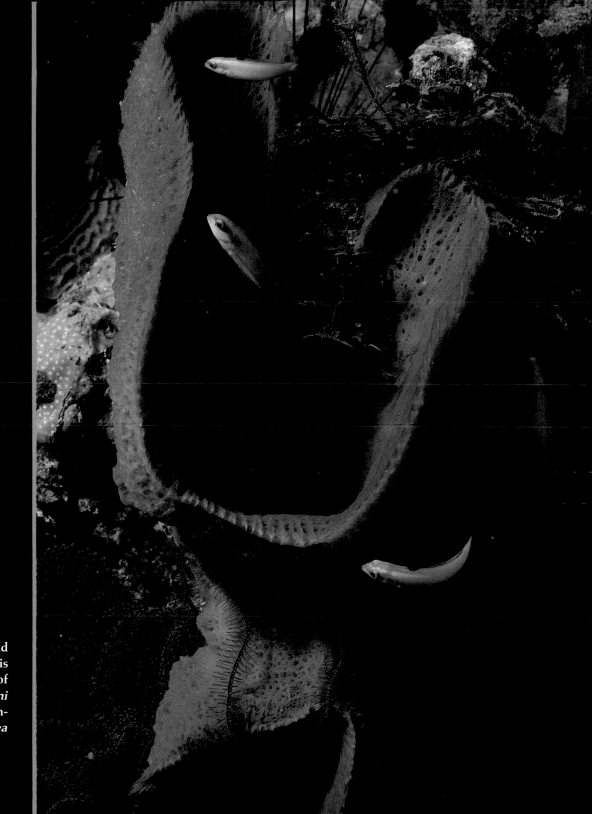

37 More intermediate-phase Bluehead wrasses (see #7) over a sponge that is probably a *Callyspongia*, with arms of the brittle star, *Ophiothrix suensoni* below and some green coral-like anemones (corallimorphs called *Ricordea florida*) in the lower left.

38 Various colored Hydrocoral from the class Hydrozoa. These corals are usually found in cryptic (cave-like) habitats.

39 *(right)* Another species of crinoid, *Nemaster discoidea*, with similar habits to *N. rubiginosa* (see #23). Shown over some retracted and some expanded polyps of the non-reef-building (i.e. ahermatypic) orange tube coral *Tubastrea aurea*.

40 The Flamingo tongue, *Cyphoma gibbosum*, a predatory snail, feeds exclusively on gorgonians, like the one shown here, probably a *Plexaura flexuosa*. Feeding scars can be seen just below the snail.

41 The Barred hamlet, *Hypoplectrus puella*; grows to c. 13 cm. Next to an
upright sponge, probably a *Verongia* or a *Callyspongia*.

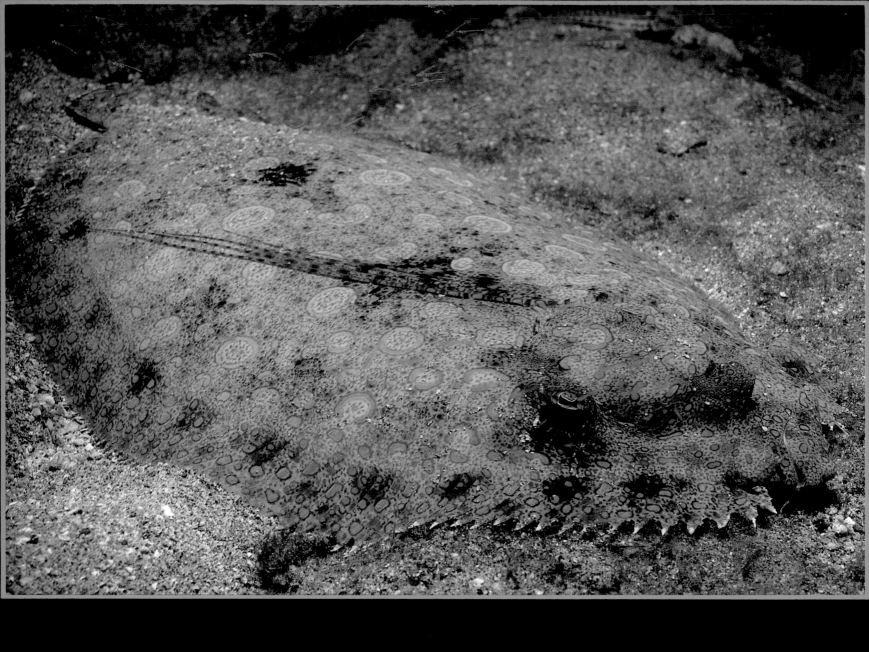

42 The Peacock flounder, *Bothus lunatus*, reaches a length of about 45 cm.

43 *(right)* A puffed-up version of the Balloonfish (or Spiny puffer), *Diodon holocanthus* (different from #36).

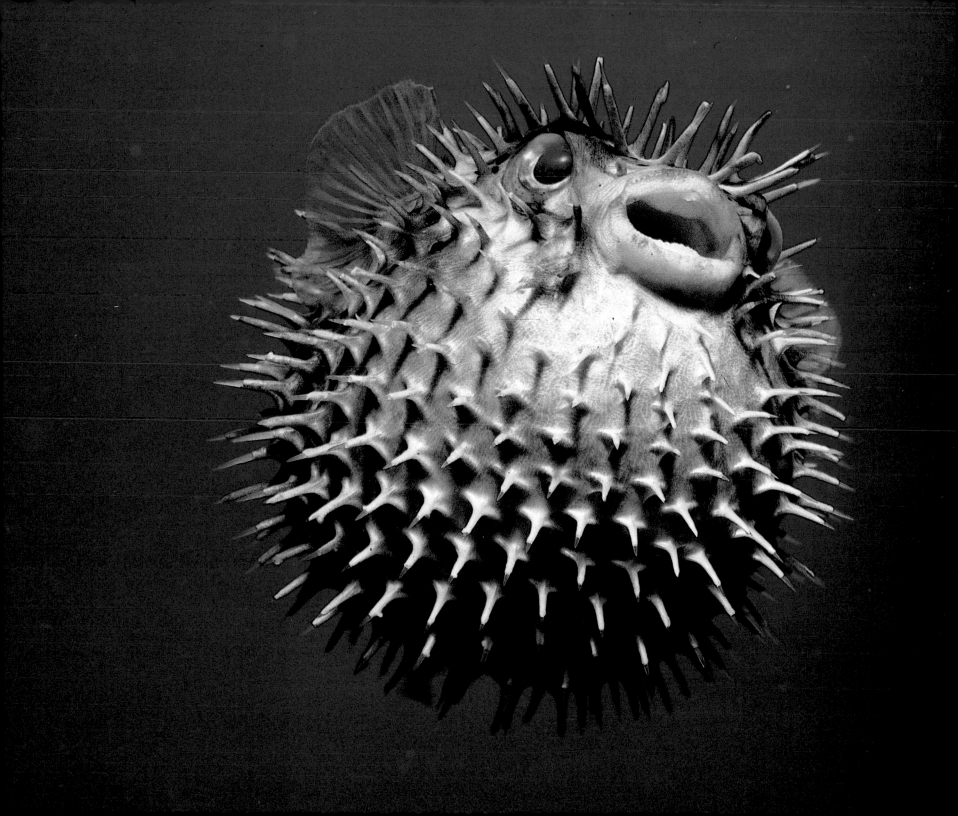

44 Large sponge, most likely a *Callyspongia*, and smaller sponges of the genus *Verongia* or *Agelus*; coral to the left is of the genus *Mycetophyllia*.

45 Sponge, possibly another *Callyspongia*; *Porites* finger coral on left and Brown chromis.

46 Diver and a school of Blue chromis, *Chromis cyaneus*, with similar habits to the Brown chromis. Also an upright sponge, *Haliclona rubens*, over an old coral head with several separated colonies of the coral, *Siderastrea*. Fire coral, *Millepora alcicornis* at lower right and the leaf coral, *Agaricia agaricites* at lower left.

47 *(right)* A cluster of the grey finger coral, *Porites* (probably *P. furcata*) in foreground and a larger accumulation of the yellow pencil coral, *Madracis mirabilis* in the background. The latter species usually grows on deeper reefs, below 15 m.

48 White specimen of the urchin, *Diadema antillarum*, with a pink sponge (probably another *Callyspongia*).

49 *(right)* Branched gorgonian, probably *Plexaura flexuosa*, with a flattened growth form, fairly typical in the Caribbean. Pink sponge is unidentifiable.

50 Lavender sponge, probably of the genus *Callyspongia* or *Dasychalina*.

51 *(right)* Unidentified sabellid feather-duster tube worms surrounding the fire coral, *Millepora alcicornis*.

52 A scuba diver peers into a cave opening; unidentifiable squirrelfish, sponges, corals, gorgonians, and other species cover the walls.

53 Yellowtail snapper, *Ocyurus chrysurus* (see #6), a Squirrelfish (un-identifiable), the purple/yellow blur of a Fairy basslet, *Gramma loreto*, in the upper right corner, and various sponges.

54 The Shy hamlet, *Hypoplectrus guttavarius*, over yellow pencil coral, *Madracis mirabilis*. The Shy hamlet is a relatively rare species and according to Randall (1968) has only been taken in the Florida Keys and six West Indian localities.

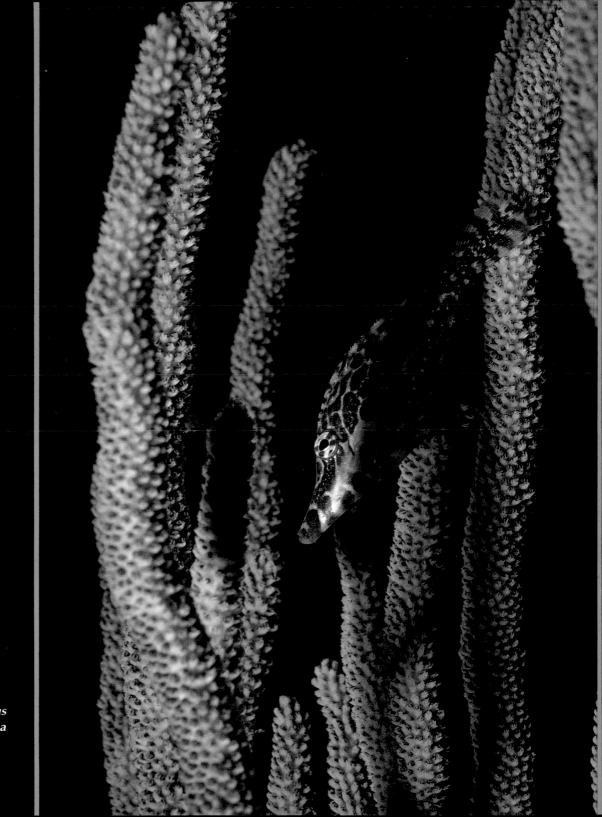

55 The Slender filefish, *Monacanthus tuckeri*, against the gorgonian, *Eunicea* sp.

56 The firecoral, *Millepora* (probably *M. complanta*) (see #7) with some
brittle star arms wrapping around colonies. Firecoral is so named for the
burning sensation caused when one brushes against it.

57 Numerous sponges (orange and lavender) with the mountainous star coral *Montastrea annularis* on the right along with the yellow/purple juvenile of the Spanish hogfish, *Bodianus rufus*, intermediate-stage Bluehead wrasses (small yellow fish) (see #7), and *Millepora* firecoral (mustard-colored colony at top).

58 This is the characteristically purple holdfast of the fan gorgonian of the genus *Gorgonia*, with small, green/brown individual feeding polyps visible. Holdfasts anchor coral to a solid base.

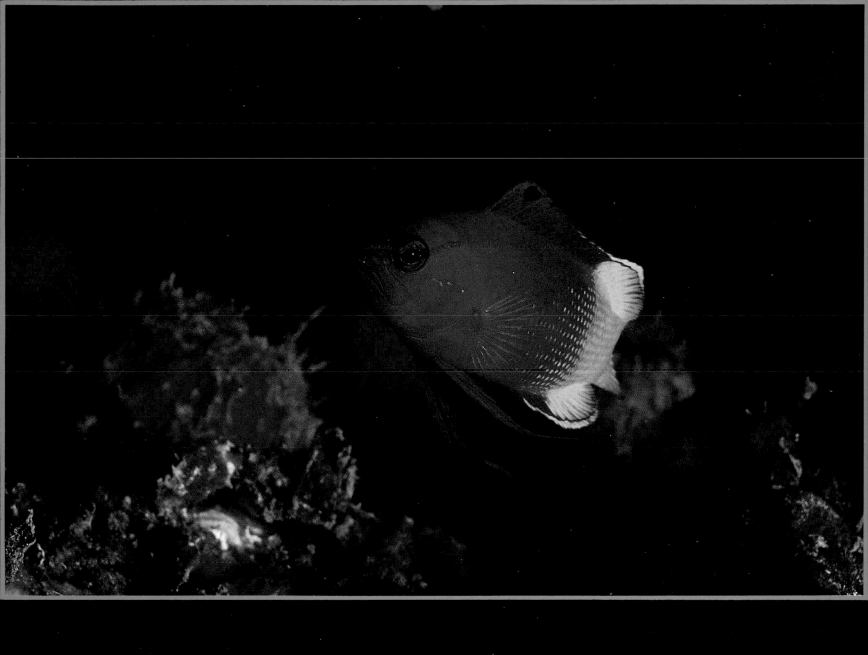

59 Fairy basslet, *Gramma loreto* (see #53). These small fish are often to be
seen swimming upside down under rocky overhangs.

60 *(left)* Arrow crab, *Stenorhynchus seticornis*, its rostrum (pointed snout) encrusted with algae, crawling on a sponge that may be the stinging sponge *Neofibularia*.

61 The French grunt, *Haemulon flavolineatum* (see #30) hanging over an orange sponge (maybe an *Agelus*) at center, with the bluish-colored large flower coral, *Mussa angulosa* and reddish upright sponge, *Haliclona rubens* (lower left); also the greenish Mustard coral, *Porites astreoides* (lower middle) and an unidentifiable bluish sponge (middle-right) parasitized by the anemone-like zoanthid, *Parazoanthus parasiticus* (small polyps on the sponge).

62 *(left)* Goldentail moray, *Muraena miliaris* (see #14) in front of the fire coral, *Millepora* and an unidentified reddish sponge.

63 Diver above the gorgonian *Plexaura* (could be *P. homomala* or *P. flexuosa*) atop a collection of the yellow-orange zoanthid, *Parazoanthus swiftii*, a parasite (see #13), and a collection of pink sponges.

64 A common reef-crevice inhabitant, the Squirrelfish, *Holocentrus rufus*, in front of a backdrop of red sponge, yellow zoanthids and bushy hydroids.

65 Diver on a reef at 12 m with the distinctive, strictly West Indian
gorgonian, *Iciligorgia schrammi*, whose colonies may reach over 2 m
across. Also seen protruding from a crevice in the reef to the right is the
crinoid, *Nemaster* (see #23).

66 Strong, penetrating rays of the Caribbean sun backlight this unidentified orange sponge.

67 The slate-pencil urchin, *Eucidaris tribuloides*, whose spines are often encrusted with fauna or flora. Here seen encrusted with an orange/brown sponge, dull reddish calcareous coralline algae and little red dots of the colonial foraminiferan *Homotrema* (a protozoan). Urchin is resting on a red sponge, possibly *Microciona*.

68 *(left)* A school of the planktivorous Creole wrasse, *Clepticus parrae;* can grow to 30 cm.

69 Diver over a fan gorgonian, *Gorgonia* (probably *G. ventalina*) behind the sponge *Haliclona rubens.*

70 Common anemone, *Condylactis gigantea* (see #4) below an unidentifiable
sponge.

71 Creole wrasse (foreground—see #68), and Brown chromis (background—see #2).

72 Diver inspects a large sea fan gorgonian, *Gorgonia* sp. and smaller branched gorgonian to the left, a *Pterogorgia* sp. and a couple of adult male or female Bluehead wrasses (see #7).

73 *(right)* A 'supermale' Bluehead wrasse at center-left (see #11) and several others of the same species (yellow—see #7) over an old dead coral mound covered now by an upright gorgonian (either of the genus *Eunicea* or *Plexaura*), the encrusting zoanthid, *Palythoa caribaeorum*, and what seems to be a dozen or more greenish colored sea anemones, *Stoichactis helianthus*. *Stoichactis* and *Palythoa* often occur in large numbers in a shallow reef site such as this. Orange sponge is unidentifiable.

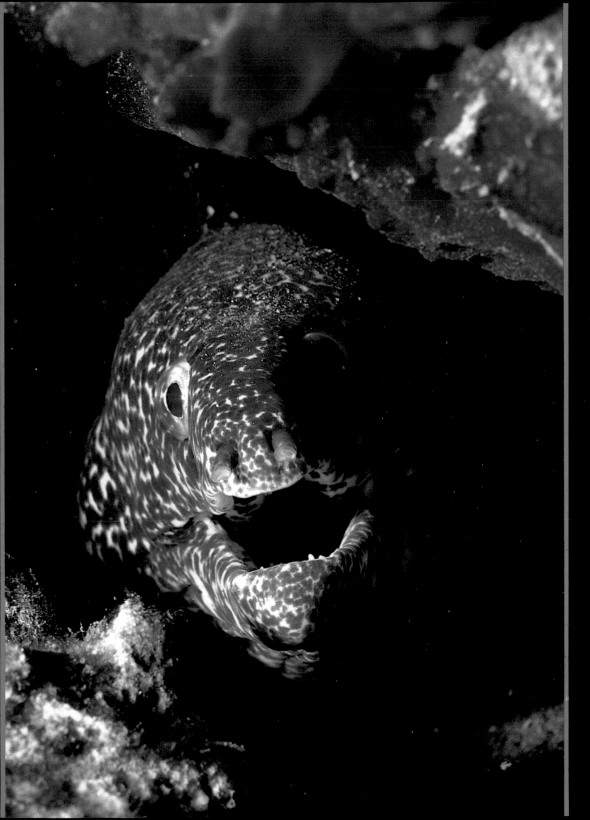

74 The spotted moray eel, *Gymnotho-rax moringa*, in its typical crevice habitat; grows to about 1.2 m and is found on both sides of the Atlantic. This is the most common moray in the West Indies.

75 Spotted scorpionfish, *Scorpaena plumieri*; grows to 45 cm. Scorpion-fishes get their name from the poisonous spines on their dorsal fins. When disturbed, they present a warning display by spreading open their strik-ingly contrasted black-and-white pectoral fins.

76 Orange tube coral, *Tubastrea aurea*
(see #39). A non-reef-building coral,
fully expanded during the day, this species prefers dimly lit conditions such as
underhangs.

77 The Bigeye, *Priacanthus arenatus*, grows to about 40 cm and is
secretive by day in reef crevices, like the squirrel fishes and cardinal fishes
it somewhat resembles. At night it comes out to feed. Shown here below
the leaf coral, *Agaricia agaricites* and above the saucer coral, *Helioseris
cucullata*.

78 *(left)* A juvenile of the Rock beauty, *Holocanthus tricolor*, a type of angelfish. This species can attain a length of 30 cm. Shown here next to the finger coral, *Porites*, a yellowish sponge (possibly an *Agelus*) and several bluish colored individuals of the sea anemones, *Stoichactis helianthus* (see #73).

79 The yellowish *Verongia* tubular sponges, probably *longissima*, growing in front of another purple sponge (possibly an *Agelus*) and over the greenish colored finger coral, *Porites*. A tiny yellow/black striped juvenile Bluehead wrasse, *Thalassoma bifasciatum*, can be seen on top of one sponge tube. Juveniles of this species are known to set up 'cleaning stations' on such promontories where they pick ecto-parasites off other fishes that come to these locations to be cleaned (see same condition in #3).

80 *(left)* Supermale of the Yellowhead wrasse, *Halichoeres garnoti* swimming over bushy hydroids.

81 Bluehead wrasses, *Thalassoma bifasciatum*, swimming past anemonelike zoanthids, *Parazoanthus*.

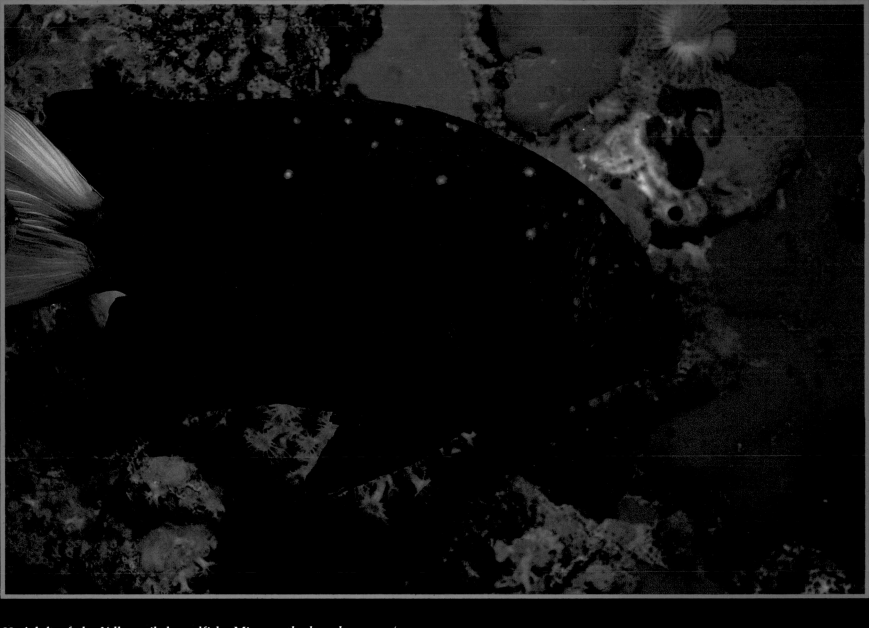

82 Adult of the Yellowtail damselfish, *Microspathodon chrysurus* (see
juvenile phase in #9) against a backdrop of unidentifiable red sponges, a
yellow sabellid fan worm and polyps of the yellow zoanthid, *Parazoanthus swiftii* below.

83 Diver with Blue chromis, *Chromis cyaneus*, swimming over a brown-colored starlet coral, *Siderastrea*, and an unidentifiable orange-lobed sponge.

84 *Condylactis gigantea* anemone in foreground; more chromis swimming over reef and maybe also some Bluehead wrasses; upright gorgonian is either a *Plexaurella* sp. or a *Briareum asbestinum*.

85 Juvenile Queen angelfish, *Holocanthus ciliaris*, surrounded by unidentified sponges.

86 Mixture of sponges and fire coral.